THE ALITALIA
BOOK OF AUTHENTIC
ITALIAN COOKING

BARBARA STACY

The Alitalia
Book of Authentic
Italian Cooking

THOMAS Y. CROWELL COMPANY

New York, Established 1834

INTRODUCTION

The versatility of Italian cookery often comes as a pleasant surprise to American tourists who have preconceived notions of Italian food. Ask most people about Italian food and a few images invariably spring to mind: spaghetti, veal cutlet enmeshed in mozzarella cheese, and pizza.

Agreed—these are delicious dishes. But they don't begin to reveal the wealth of one of the world's great cuisines.

Perhaps the fact that most Italians who emigrated to America came from southern Italy accounts for the stubborn popularity of a few dishes. They introduced only their own regional favorites. Southern Italians brought with them enthusiastic regard for the garlic clove, olive oil, and the tomato—tastes shared with more restraint by the northerners.

In Italy, garlic generally decreases in popularity as it travels north. Southerners dispense it with a lavish hand; in the middle regions, it goes into food with moderation; northern Italians use garlic sparingly (except in Genoa).

In the south, olive oil invariably goes into the frying pan; in the north, butter. Little more than halfway up the Boot, around Tuscany, the housewife fries food impartially in equal amounts of olive oil and butter. Tuscany is the Mason-Dixon Line separating the olive oil and butter belts.

The tomato, too, decreases in regard as it travels north. Sicilians, in the southernmost region, frequently serve pasta (any of the varied macaroni products, including spaghetti) with tomato sauce. The sauce is of incomparable richness, having been combined with a judicious assortment of herbs and spices, and simmered until evaporation leaves a thick essence. Further north, other sauces go over pasta: *pesto,* a savory combination of garlic and basil, or sauce *alla Bolognese,* made of ground meat, or melted butter and freshly grated cheese.

With the few exceptions noted here, ingredients used in Italian cookery can be purchased everywhere. You may have trouble finding prosciutto, the wafer-thin spiced ham that often adds flavor to vegetables or other meats. When there's none to be had, don't abandon the recipe; substitute boiled ham or thinly sliced Canadian bacon.

Truffles, the underground fungi of superb flavor, have been eliminated from the recipes that follow, although they frequently appear in Italian cookery. Fresh white Italian truffles are not available here.

Fresh herbs (especially marjoram, orégano, and basil) go into many Italian dishes. But since they are hard to come by in America, the quantities called for refer to dried herbs. Fresh herbs unquestionably have better flavor, however; if you can, get them fresh and step up the quantity to taste.

Since most cooks don't keep homemade chicken broth or beef broth at hand, broth-based soups and stews can be made with canned broth, or with chicken or beef bouillon cubes.

The recipes that follow are, to my mind, the cream of Italian cuisine. Try, for instance, Saltimbocca, thin veal cutlets rolled with prosciutto slices and sautéed in butter; Fritto Misto, a delicious mixture of meats and vegetables, all deep fried; Gnocchi, tiny potato dumplings to be served with melted butter and grated Parmesan cheese or sauce; Zabaglione, a dessert composed chiefly of beaten egg yolk, Marsala wine, and air. They're all superb; they're all Italian cookery at its most elegant.

I would like to thank the personnel of Alitalia Airlines, and Mr. Francesco Vinci in particular, for their help in compiling this book.

Buon appetito!

ITALY ALOFT

Last year, 951,000 Americans visited Italy—and as many fell in love with this incomparably charming country. Some tourists preferred the splendor of Rome, with its combination of ancient treasures and modern fast-paced excitement. Others became enamored of Venice, for to visit this exquisite storybook city is to be magically catapulted five hundred years back in time. For the art lover, Florence is paradise. And the tourist who goes to Europe to seek the bright sun and blue sea becomes enchanted with Capri or the Italian Riviera.

These are the places most visited by the American, but Italy's riches don't stop here. The more adventurous visitor finds that Italy abounds with areas more off the beaten track that offer a wealth of art, architecture, and charming villages where the tourist is greeted with the warmth and geniality characteristic of the Italian people.

Many tourists begin their trip to Italy at New York's International Airport when they board an Alitalia jet, for Alitalia's planes are truly "Italy aloft."

The graciousness of Italian hospitality is immediately apparent; to the Italian host the comfort of his guest is all important—and the airline reflects this agreeable philosophy. The cabins are spacious and luxurious, fresh flowers greet the traveler in the lounge, Italian music fills the air, and contemporary Italian paintings decorate the walls. With the handsomeness and luxury of the surroundings goes service calculated to make each guest feel he is receiving a royal treatment.

Alitalia Airlines is particularly proud of its food, skillfully prepared in the Old World tradition and served with the noblest of champagne and vintage wines.

First Class meals are served on dainty gold-rimmed china bearing Alitalia's Winged Arrow crest. Sterling silver flatware, sparkling crystal, and fine linen all add to the atmosphere of elegance. As for the service, Alitalia's stewards have been trained in Europe's most exclusive hotels.

When it comes to food, Alitalia offers cuisine that would do credit to a deluxe hotel. The company insists that all ingredients be of excellent quality—the finest that money can buy. Choice meats, vegetables, fish, sauces, and desserts are then carefully prepared in the Old World tradition by expert Italian chefs, according to menus worked out in the food department at Rome.

The whole food operation aboard Alitalia planes is a miracle of efficiency, and the chief miracle-worker is Mr. Pietro Drago, who supervises operations at International Airport with the utmost skill. Here is how Mr. Drago goes about his incredibly complicated job.

Each jet that takes off for Italy holds about 150 passengers, and each passenger is provided with one hot meal and one cold meal. During the height of the tourist season,

Mr. Drago may be called upon to provide food for over 600 passengers in a single day.

The food is partially cooked in the huge commissary at International Airport. Then it is loaded on small metal trays and the trays are stacked in large insulated metal containers. The containers are then whisked aboard the jet and stored in two galleys: one is for First Class service, the other for Economy service. And here is where the magic comes in. Each galley is about six feet square—or a size that would mean despair for the housewife who had to prepare company dinner for four!

Because of its brilliantly compact design, there is room for everything with not one square inch left over! The small trays of food slip into the same size drawers in the refrigerator or in the wall ovens, depending upon whether the food is to be chilled or heated.

At meal time, the food is stacked on carts and served by the stewards.

The food is, of course, generally Italian, but other Continental dishes, cooked with Italian flair, may be served. The First Class passenger may receive a succulent *filet mignon* topped with a thin layer of truffle-flecked *pâté de foie gras*. The Economy Class passenger will have a more modest dish, but one that has been prepared with the same amount of loving care: chicken cacciatora, for instance, which is made with a delicate tomato sauce, or chicken alla diavola, prepared in a spicier tomato sauce.

Inevitably, excellent pasta takes its place on the menu. Mr. Drago favors cannelloni, wide stuffed noodles, or tortellini, tiny rounds of pasta that are absolutely delectable. For dessert, you may be served pan di Spagna, a Strega-flavored spongecake, or cassata, the classical fluffy cheesecake made with ricotta cheese.

A typical midnight supper served to First Class passengers on Alitalia's jetliners bound from New York to Rome starts with cocktails and includes caviar, truffled *pâté de foie gras,* stuffed tomatoes, seafood patties, chicken galantine, *filet mignon,* assorted cheeses, pastry, fresh fruit, coffee, and liqueurs. Champagne, of course, accompanies the meal.

Whether the tourist travels First Class or Economy Class, his transatlantic trip by Alitalia Airlines will be a glimpse of Italy aloft.

CONTENTS

ANTIPASTO

A colorful antipasto, "before the food,"
raises the curtain for the Italian dinner.
Antipasto can be any hors d'oeuvre. But
the classic Italian Antipasto is a cold
platter composed of a variety of cold
sausages. Other favorite antipasto dishes
are the delicious prosciutto of Parma
combined with melon or fresh figs, cold
vegetables marinated in olive oil or
vinegar, or seafood prepared in a variety
of fashions.

Some of the following recipes can do
double duty as a salad course.

Italian-American Antipasto

Because Italian-Americans were not able to purchase the wide variety of delicious spicy sausages available in Italy for Antipasto, other foods found their way to the cold "before the food" appetizer.

The Antipasto plate contains any combination of the following:

Italian salami
Prosciutto
Olives
Celery
Fried peppers (see index)
Capers
Hard-cooked egg slices
Boiled beans
Pimiento
Radishes
Tuna
Sardines
Anchovies
Whole shrimps or mussels
Lettuce
Endive
Tomatoes

Arrange the assortment on individual serving plates and accompany with olive oil and vinegar.

Prosciutto and Melon

PROSCIUTTO CON MELONE

2 small cantaloupes, or 1 honeydew,
    previously chilled
¼ pound prosciutto

Peel the melons and cut them into thin wedges. Arrange the wedges in the center of a platter with the pieces over-lapping, and place a row of prosciutto around the border, each slice folded in half. SERVES 4.

If preferred, peeled fresh figs may be substituted for the melon.

Stuffed Eggs with Spinach

UOVA SODE CON SPINACI

½ pound spinach, cooked and chopped
½ package cream cheese
 2 tablespoons grated Parmesan cheese
 8 hard-cooked eggs
 1 tablespoon chopped parsley
   Salt
   Pepper
½ teaspoon nutmeg

Cut the hard-cooked eggs in half and remove yolks. Mash the spinach well with cream cheese, Parmesan cheese, the egg yolks, parsley, salt, and pepper. Stuff the egg whites with the mixture, piling it high, and sprinkle with nutmeg. SERVES 4.

Stuffed Peppers

PEPERONI RIPIENI

4 large peppers
8 tablespoons olive oil
2 cups bread crumbs
4 anchovies, chopped
2 tablespoons chopped black olives
8 pimiento strips

1 tablespoon chopped parsley
½ tablespoon capers

Remove the tops of the peppers and scrape out the seeds.
In a skillet, heat 2 tablespoons oil; then add bread crumbs
and brown. Add anchovies, olives, pimiento, parsley, and
capers; heat and then stuff the peppers with this mixture.
Pour 2 tablespoons olive oil in a baking pan, arrange
peppers in pan, and sprinkle 1 tablespoon olive oil on
each pepper. Bake the peppers in a slow oven, 325° F.,
for 40 minutes, or until they are done. They can be served
cold or hot. SERVES 4.

Cold Veal with Tuna Sauce

VITELLO TONNATO

2-pound leg of veal, boned and rolled
4 anchovies
1 onion, stuck with 2 cloves
1 bay leaf
1 stalk celery
1 tablespoon chopped parsley
  Salt
  Pepper
3½ ounces tuna, canned in olive oil
  Juice of 1 lemon
2 teaspoons capers
3 tablespoons olive oil
1 lemon, sliced

Cut incisions in the veal and insert in them pieces of 2 anchovies. Simmer the veal, covered, in 4 cups water with the onion, bay leaf, celery, parsley, salt, and pepper for 1½ hours, or until the meat is tender. Cool the meat, cut it into thin slices, pack it in a bowl, and cover it with the following sauce:

Mash the tuna with the oil from the can, mash in the remaining anchovies, and add the lemon juice and capers. Add enough of the olive oil to make a sauce about the consistency of thin mayonnaise. Let the dish marinate in the refrigerator for 2 days. Serve the veal on a platter with the tuna sauce and garnish with thin lemon slices. SERVES 8.

Chicken Liver Canapés

CROSTINI DI FEGATO
DI POLLO

1 small white onion, minced
2 stalks celery, chopped
1 tablespoon olive oil
6 chicken livers
½ cup mushrooms, thinly sliced
½ cup hot chicken broth
1 tablespoon bread crumbs
  Juice of ½ lemon
1 small loaf Italian bread, thinly sliced and
    toasted

Sauté the onion and celery in olive oil for 10 minutes, or until the celery is tender. Add the livers and mushrooms; cook for 5 minutes longer. Slice the livers and mash the mixture. Add hot broth, bread crumbs, and lemon juice, mixing well. Chill the liver paste and serve it on thin rounds of toast. SERVES 4.

Eggplant Relish

CAPONATINA

    4 eggplants, peeled and diced
1½ cups olive oil
    3 onions, sliced
    2 tomatoes, diced
    3 stalks celery, diced
    1 can tomato paste
    3 tablespoons capers
  10 green olives, pitted and diced
    2 tablespoons pine nuts
  ½ cup wine vinegar
    2 tablespoons sugar
      Salt
      Pepper

Fry the eggplant in 1 cup hot olive oil for 5 minutes, or until it is brown. Remove the eggplant and add the remaining oil and onions. Cook the onions until they are golden, then add tomatoes, celery, and tomato paste, and cook until the celery is tender, adding water if necessary. Return the fried eggplant to the pan, add the remaining ingredients, and simmer for 20 minutes, stirring frequently. Pour the relish into warm sterile jars and seal with paraffin. Cool and chill. Caponatina keeps well indefinitely in the refrigerator.

Marinated Artichoke Hearts

CARCIOFINI PER ANTIPASTO

½ cup olive oil
2 tablespoons lemon juice
¼ teaspoon orégano
  Salt
  Pepper
1 box frozen artichoke hearts, cooked and
    cooled

Combine the olive oil, lemon juice, and seasoning. Add the artichokes and marinate in the refrigerator for at least 3 hours, stirring occasionally. SERVES 4.

Oysters with Caviar

OSTRICHE ALLA VENEZIANA

2 dozen oysters
Juice of 2 lemons
Freshly ground black pepper
½ cup caviar
1 lemon, cut in wedges
Parsley sprigs

Remove the top shells and leave the oysters in the deeper shells. Sprinkle lightly with lemon juice and pepper and surround the oyster in each shell with a border of caviar. Arrange the oysters on plates of cracked ice, garnish each dish with lemon wedges and parsley sprigs. SERVES 4.

SOUPS

Centuries ago, when inns in Italy were scarce, monks offered hospitality to the traveler. To make sure the monastery kitchen would be ready for unexpected guests at all times, the brothers always kept a special "soup for guests" on the fire. Into this kettle went beef, vegetables, pasta, beans, and seasonings. This was minestra. *We now call a similar version* minestrone, *or large* minestra—*and it is the most famous of Italian soups.*

Italian soups range from hearty minestrone to delicate green soup. Sprinkle the soups with grated Parmesan and serve with crusty Italian bread or with bread sticks.

Minestrone

Minestrone, like Fritto Misto (see index), can be composed of a variety of ingredients, depending on the yield of the cupboard. It is made of beef, vegetables, beans, and pasta or rice. Use some or all of the ingredients suggested below, or substitute those of your own choice. Whatever you use, cook the soup long and slowly.

2 onions, chopped
2 tablespoons olive oil
2 pounds soup beef
2 stalks celery, with leaves
1 cup chopped zucchini
1 cup chopped green beans
1 cup chopped tomatoes
1 cup sliced carrots
1 cup shredded cabbage
1 cup dried beans or chick peas, soaked
    overnight in water to cover
1 clove garlic, minced
½ cup chopped fresh parsley
2 cups small pasta (spaghetti or macaroni,
    broken in small pieces; pastina; or tiny
    stars or squares)

1 cup grated Parmesan cheese
Salt
Pepper

In a heavy kettle, sauté the onions in olive oil until they are golden. Add the meat, 3½ quarts water, and celery. Bring water to a boil; skim. Cook meat, covered, over low heat for 2½ hours, adding liquid as necessary. Add vegetables, garlic, and parsley and cook for ½ hour longer, or until vegetables are tender. Parboil pasta for 6 minutes; drain and add to soup with cheese, salt, and pepper. Cook rapidly for 5 minutes longer; lower the heat and cook soup for 5 minutes more. Remove meat and cut it into shreds. Put a few shreds in each soup bowl, add the soup, and sprinkle with grated cheese. SERVES 8.

Anchovy Soup with Rice

MINESTRA ALLA CAPPUCCINA

1 onion, chopped
4 tablespoons butter
3 anchovies, mashed
2 cups cooked rice
6 cups beef broth
2 teaspoons chopped parsley
Pepper
4 slices toasted Italian bread
2 tablespoons grated Parmesan cheese

Sauté onion in butter until it is golden and then add all ingredients but toast and grated Parmesan cheese. Simmer the soup for 30 minutes. Put toast in bowls and pour the soup over it. Sprinkle with grated Parmesan cheese. SERVES 4.

Bean and Pasta Soup

PASTA E FAGIOLI

1 beef marrowbone
1 cup dried white beans, soaked in water to
    cover overnight
2 tablespoons chopped white pork fat
1 onion, chopped
  Salt
  Pepper
2 cloves garlic, split
1 tablespoon chopped parsley
½ teaspoon rosemary
3 tablespoons olive oil
1 tablespoon tomato paste, diluted in ⅓ cup
    warm water
1 cup *ditalini* (small macaroni)

Cook marrowbone, beans, pork fat, chopped onion, salt, and pepper in 3½ quarts water, covered, for 1½ hours. Sauté garlic, parsley, and rosemary in olive oil, stirring

constantly. Cook for 5 minutes longer; add tomato paste
and simmer for 10 minutes, stirring frequently. Discard
garlic and add sauce to beans with salt and pepper. Simmer for 2 hours more, or until beans are soft, adding
more water if necessary. Remove the bone, add the macaroni, and cook for 12 minutes longer, stirring occasionally.
SERVES 8.

Cabbage and Rice Soup Lombardy

VERZATA DI RISO
ALLA LOMBARDA

3 strips bacon, diced
3 tomatoes, peeled and chopped
1 green pepper, chopped
1 clove garlic, split
1 tablespoon chopped parsley
1 small cabbage, shredded
2 quarts beef broth
  Salt
  Pepper
1 cup rice
⅓ cup grated Parmesan cheese

Fry bacon in butter until it is golden; add tomatoes, green
pepper, garlic, and parsley. Simmer for 15 minutes; discard garlic and add cabbage. Simmer, covered, for 15

minutes more. Add broth, salt, and pepper, and simmer, covered, for 1 hour. Add more liquid if necessary. Add rice and simmer, covered, for 20 minutes more, or until rice is done. Sprinkle with grated Parmesan cheese. SERVES 6.

Egg Drop Soup

STRACCIATELLE

2 eggs, separated
3 tablespoons grated Parmesan cheese
¼ teaspoon nutmeg
6 cups chicken broth

Beat egg whites until they are nearly stiff; fold in the yolks, cheese, and nutmeg. Bring the broth to a boil and add the egg mixture slowly, stirring constantly. Simmer soup for 5 minutes over low heat, still stirring. SERVES 4.

Poached Eggs in Broth

ZUPPA ALLA PAVESE

4 thin slices Italian bread, fried in butter
4 eggs

2 tablespoons grated Parmesan cheese
6 cups chicken broth

Place fried bread slices in 4 small casseroles. Place an egg on top of each slice, being careful not to break the yolk, and sprinkle with grated Parmesan. Carefully pour the broth over the eggs and bake in a moderate oven, 350° F., for 8 minutes, or until the eggs are lightly poached. SERVES 4.

Green Soup

ZUPPA DI VERDURA

2 cups chopped spinach
1 head lettuce, shredded
1 stalk celery, chopped
6 cups chicken broth
  Salt
  Pepper
¼ cup grated Parmesan cheese

Combine all ingredients except grated Parmesan cheese and simmer for 30 minutes. If desired, ingredients may then be forced through a sieve or puréed in a blender. Sprinkle with grated Parmesan cheese. SERVES 4.

Cream of Potato Soup

ZUPPA DI PATATE

3 slices bacon, minced
2 pounds potatoes, diced
2 onions, sliced
2 cups beef broth
2½ cups hot milk
   Salt
   Pepper
2 teaspoons chopped parsley

Place bacon, potatoes, and onions in a kettle with the broth and bring the soup to a boil. Cover the kettle and simmer the soup for 30 minutes. Remove the potatoes and purée them. Mix the purée into the broth; add the milk, salt, and pepper, mixing well. Simmer over low heat until the soup is hot, being careful not to let it come to a boil. Sprinkle with parsley. SERVES 4.

PASTA,
PASTA SAUCES,
RICE, AND
CORN MEAL

When the antipasto is not followed by a soup, Italians serve pasta, polenta, risotto, or a similar dish before the main course. Each region has its favorite.

The Milanese, who lives in the rice belt, prefers risotto—rice cooked in broth and flavored with saffron. He serves it as a separate course or with Osso Buco (see index). The Venetian farmer likes his polenta—corn meal—boiled, baked, or fried and served unaccompanied or with sauce. He often eats it with veal birds, too.

But from Rome southward, pasta rules the gastronomic roost. According to one authority, there are more than 350 kinds of pasta in Italy, many with fanciful names. You can eat stelline, *or little stars;*

farfalle, *or bows;* occhi di lupo, *or wolf's eyes;* ombrelli, *or tiny umbrellas. If you are of a mechanical turn of mind, you can have in your soup* radiatori, *or little radiators. Or if something more divine suits your fancy, choose* capelli d'angelo, *or angel's hair, a very delicate pasta.*

Green Noodles

4 cups sifted flour
1 teaspoon salt
2 eggs, beaten
¾ cup spinach purée
1 cup (½ pound) sweet butter
1 cup grated Parmesan cheese
   Freshly ground black pepper

Sift the flour with the salt to form a mound on a pastry board. Make a well in the center of the mound and pour into it the eggs and spinach purée. Combine the ingredients to form a rather stiff dough, adding a little water if necessary. Turn the dough out on a floured board and roll it into a very thin rectangle. Roll the dough up firmly and slice it crosswise in narrow strips. Arrange the strips on the board in a single layer and let them dry for about 2 hours. Cook the noodles in a generous amount of rapidly boiling salted water for 8 minutes, or until they are just tender. Drain well and mix with the butter, grated cheese, and pepper. Serve with more butter and grated cheese on the side. SERVES 4.

Macaroni with Ricotta Cheese

PASTA CON RICOTTA

1 pound macaroni, any type
1 pound ricotta or cottage cheese
½ cup milk
½ teaspoon nutmeg
3 tablespoons butter
½ cup grated Parmesan cheese
  Salt
  Pepper
1 tablespoon chopped parsley

Cook macaroni according to directions on package until it is just tender. Drain, return to pan, and add butter. Mix ricotta with milk and nutmeg; add ricotta mixture to macaroni and cook, covered, over low heat for 5 minutes. Add grated cheese, salt, and pepper and sprinkle with parsley. SERVES 4.

Ravioli

A great rivalry exists among the various regions of Italy involving the most excellent filling for ravioli. In Italy, ravioli often appear in broth, or with butter and grated cheese, as a change from tomato sauce. Either style permits you to savor fully the delicate stuffing. If you've never eaten ravioli in this simple fashion, it will be a revelation.

> 6 cups flour, sifted
> 1 teaspoon salt
> 6 eggs, beaten

Add salt to flour and arrange in a mound on a pastry board sprinkled with flour. Make a well in the center and pour in the beaten eggs and 1 tablespoon lukewarm water. With a spoon, carefully work the flour into the liquid little by little to form a stiff dough. If the dough is too thick, add a little water; if it is too thin, sift in a little more flour.

Knead the dough into a ball and set it aside for 30 minutes. Divide dough into two parts and roll it out on a floured board into two sheets. Place teaspoonfuls of stuffing on one sheet at intervals of 1½ inches; cover with second sheet of dough and press firmly around each mold with your fingers. Cut the ravioli into 2-inch squares with a pastry cutter.

Let the ravioli stand for 30 minutes and then boil them in water or broth for 10 minutes, or until they rise to the top. Remove them with a slotted spoon and serve in broth as a soup (SERVES 8); or drained, with butter and grated cheese or any pasta sauce. SERVES 4.

Meat Filling for Ravioli

RIPIENO DI CARNE
PER RAVIOLI

1 pound cooked meat, ground (chicken,
   pork, veal, beef, or a combination)
2 eggs, beaten
1 tablespoon chopped parsley
¼ teaspoon nutmeg
   Salt
   Pepper

Mix all ingredients well and use to fill ravioli dough as
directed.

Cheese Filling for Ravioli

RIPIENO DI FORMAGGIO
PER RAVIOLI

1 pound ricotta or cottage cheese
4 eggs, beaten
¼ teaspoon nutmeg
2 tablespoons grated Parmesan cheese
1 tablespoon chopped parsley

Mix all ingredients well and use to fill ravioli dough as
directed.

Shells with Sausage

PASTA CON SALSICCIA

1 pound Italian sweet sausages, skinned and
    cut in 1-inch pieces
3 tablespoons olive oil
1 onion, chopped
1 pound mushrooms, chopped
1 bay leaf
1 clove garlic
  Salt
  Pepper
2 cups tomato sauce
1 pound shells
¼ cup grated Parmesan cheese

Brown sausages in olive oil for 10 minutes; add onion, mushrooms, bay leaf, garlic, salt, and pepper and simmer for 15 minutes. Add tomato sauce and cook for 30 minutes. Discard bay leaf. Cook shells according to package directions, drain, and arrange in a baking dish. Add sausage and sauce, mix well, and sprinkle with grated Parmesan cheese. Bake in a moderate oven, 350° F., for 10 minutes, or until the top is brown. SERVES 4.

Spaghetti with Bacon Sauce

SPAGHETTI ALLA CARBONARA

8 slices bacon, finely chopped
1 pound spaghetti
4 eggs
1 cup grated Parmesan cheese
  Pepper

Sauté bacon in a skillet until it is golden; do not let it become crisp. Cook the spaghetti according to directions on package, drain well, and return to saucepan. Combine the eggs with the grated cheese and beat the mixture. Add the eggs and cheese to the spaghetti; add the bacon and pour the hot bacon fat over the mixture, mixing well. The eggs should be lightly cooked by contact with the hot fat and hot spaghetti. If the eggs still look raw after mixing well, place the saucepan over low heat for a few minutes, stirring constantly. SERVES 4.

Spaghetti with Bacon and Tomato Sauce

SPAGHETTI
ALL'AMATRICIANA

3 tablespoons chopped onion
¼ pound bacon, chopped
½ tablespoon olive oil
1½ pounds Italian plum tomatoes, peeled
　　　　and chopped
Salt
Pepper
1 pound spaghetti
1 cup grated Pecorino or Parmesan cheese

Sauté the onion and bacon in olive oil until they are golden. Add tomatoes, salt, and pepper, and cook over high heat for 10 minutes. Meanwhile, cook the spaghetti according to directions on package and drain well. Serve the sauce over the spaghetti and sprinkle with cheese. SERVES 4.

Spaghetti with Meat Balls

SPAGHETTI CON POLPETTE

This is the classic Italian-American favorite.

½ pound beef, ground
¼ pound pork, ground
¼ pound veal, ground
1 clove garlic, minced
1 tablespoon marjoram
½ cup bread crumbs
¼ cup milk
1 egg, beaten
Salt
Pepper
4 tablespoons flour
4 tablespoons olive oil
1 onion, chopped
2½ cups (20-ounce can) Italian tomatoes
1 tablespoon chopped parsley
1 teaspoon orégano
3 tablespoons tomato paste
1 pound spaghetti
½ cup grated Parmesan cheese

Combine meat, garlic, marjoram, bread crumbs, milk, egg, salt, and pepper; mix well and form into 8 balls.

Dredge meat balls in flour and brown in olive oil. Remove the meat balls from the skillet. In the same skillet, brown onion until golden, add tomatoes, parsley, orégano, salt, and pepper and simmer for 30 minutes. Blend in tomato paste; return meat balls to sauce and simmer for 20 minutes longer. Meanwhile, cook the spaghetti according to directions on package and drain well. Pour sauce over spaghetti and serve with grated Parmesan cheese. SERVES 6.

Clam Sauce for Spaghetti or Linguine

SALSA DI VONGOLE

1 clove garlic, minced
½ cup olive oil
2½ cups (20-ounce can) Italian tomatoes
  Salt
  Pepper
1 quart cherrystone clams, in shell
1 tablespoon chopped parsley

Sauté the garlic in oil until the garlic is golden. Add tomatoes, salt, and pepper and cook for 20 minutes. Shell the clams and add them whole to sauce. Cook for 10 minutes; add parsley and serve over spaghetti or linguine. SERVES 4.

Garlic and Basil Sauce

PESTO ALLA GENOVESE

    5 cloves garlic, chopped
    ½ cup chopped fresh basil
    ⅓ cup grated Pecorino or Parmesan cheese
      Salt
      Pepper
    1 cup olive oil
    2 tablespoons butter

Put garlic, basil, cheese, salt, and pepper in a mortar and
pound to a paste. Add olive oil and butter and stir vigor-
ously. Serve over spaghetti. SERVES 4.

Tomato Sauce

SALSA DI POMODORO

The longer the ingredients blend, the more flavor for your
tomato sauce. It tastes best of all if you make it the day
before and reheat it at serving time.

    2 cloves garlic, minced
    3 tablespoons olive oil

    2 tablespoons chopped parsley
2½ cups (20-ounce can) Italian tomatoes
    2 tablespoons tomato paste
    Salt
    Pepper
1 teaspoon orégano

Sauté the garlic in olive oil for 2 minutes, stirring frequently. Add all ingredients and simmer, covered, for 1 hour, stirring from time to time. Force the sauce through a sieve and serve over spaghetti or other pasta. SERVES 4.

Marinara Sauce

SALSA ALLA MARINARA

This is essentially the same sauce as Salsa di Pomodoro, but it cooks for a shorter time and is consequently of lighter consistency.

Use the same ingredients as for Salsa di Pomodoro (above). Sauté the garlic in olive oil for 2 minutes, stirring frequently. Add 1 tablespoon parsley, reserving the remainder, and the other ingredients. Simmer for 20 minutes, add the reserved parsley, and serve over spaghetti or other pasta. (If desired, olives, mushrooms, or clams may be added.) SERVES 4.

Meat Sauce

SUGO DI CARNE

        1 clove garlic, split in half
      ¼ cup olive oil
        1 onion, chopped
        1 green pepper, chopped
      ½ pound beef, ground
      ¼ pound pork, ground
      ¼ pound veal, ground
        2 sweet Italian sausages, removed from
             their casings and chopped
   2½ cups (20-ounce can) Italian tomatoes,
             strained
        1 can tomato paste
      ½ cup dry red wine
      ¼ teaspoon orégano
        Salt
        Pepper

Sauté the garlic in olive oil until it is golden and discard the garlic. In the same oil, sauté the onion and green pepper until the onion is golden. Add the meat and brown it, separating it with a fork as it cooks. In another pan, bring the strained tomatoes and the tomato paste to a boil over low heat. Add the meat mixture, wine, and seasoning, and simmer over low heat for 2 hours, stirring occasionally. If necessary, add a little water. SERVES 4.

Lasagne

2 sweet Italian sausages, chopped
1 onion, minced
2½ cups (20-ounce can) Italian tomatoes
1 teaspoon basil
1 tablespoon chopped parsley
Salt
Pepper
1 pound lasagne or broadest noodles
available, cooked
1 pound ricotta or creamed cottage cheese
½ cup grated Parmesan cheese

Fry sausages for 3 minutes and drain most fat. Add onion and sauté until golden. Add tomatoes, ½ cup boiling water, basil, parsley, salt, and pepper; simmer, covered, for 3 hours, stirring from time to time. Place a layer of lasagne on the bottom of a buttered baking dish and pour a little sauce over it. Mix the ricotta with 2 tablespoons water and spread a few tablespoons of the mixture over the sauce. Sprinkle with some grated Parmesan cheese. Repeat the process until all these ingredients are used, ending with a layer of grated Parmesan cheese. Bake the lasagne in a moderate oven, 350° F., for 30 minutes, or until it is done. SERVES 4.

Manicotti

CANNELLONI

2 cups sifted flour
1 tablespoon butter
3 eggs
    Salt
1 pound ricotta cheese
2 cups tomato sauce
1 tablespoon chopped parsley
½ cup grated Parmesan or Romano cheese

Combine the flour, butter, eggs, and salt; gradually add ¼ cup lukewarm water and mix to form a rather soft dough. Knead the dough until it is smooth and roll it on a floured board until it is thin. Cut the dough into rectangles 4 by 6 inches. Place 1½ tablespoons ricotta in the center of each rectangle, and roll up the dough. Moisten the edges of the dough and press them firmly together to prevent the cheese from falling out. Simmer the Cannelloni for 10 minutes in a large amount of boiling water, and remove them carefully with a slotted spoon. Place the Cannelloni in a large casserole, cover with tomato sauce, and sprinkle with parsley. Bake the Cannelloni in a hot oven, 400° F., for 15 minutes. Serve with grated cheese. SERVES 4.

Corn Meal Mush

POLENTA

Polenta can be served simply, as directed below, or you can cool the cooked corn meal, slice it, and then fry, toast, or bake it.

2 cups yellow corn meal
1 tablespoon salt
½ cup (¼ pound) butter
¼ cup grated Parmesan cheese

Bring 2 quarts salted water to a boil and gradually pour in the corn meal, stirring well. Cook the corn meal, stirring constantly, for 30 minutes, or until it reaches the consistency of mashed potatoes. Stir in the butter and grated cheese. Turn the polenta into a buttered serving dish. Serve the polenta very hot with any pasta sauce. If you choose, it may also be served cold with hot pasta sauce or simply with melted butter and grated cheese. SERVES 4.

Potato Dumplings

GNOCCHI

    4 large potatoes
    1 egg yolk, beaten
    1 teaspoon salt
    ½ cup sifted flour
    4 tablespoons melted butter
    3 tablespoons grated Parmesan cheese

Boil the potatoes and mash them. Add egg yolks and 1
teaspoon salt, beating well. Gradually add flour, using
just enough to form a dough; you may not need the whole
½ cup. Knead the dough well; break off pieces and roll
them out 1½ inches long and ¾ inch wide. Add remaining
salt to a kettle of boiling water and drop in the gnocchi,
about 10 at a time. When they pop to the surface, remove
them with a slotted spoon; drain them and keep them warm.
Proceed in this fashion until all gnocchi are cooked. Arrange in a serving dish and sprinkle with melted butter
and grated Parmesan cheese. Gnocchi may also be served
with Tomato Sauce (see index). SERVES 4.

Rice with Saffron

RISOTTO ALLA MILANESE

1 onion, chopped
⅓ cup beef marrow
6 tablespoons butter
1 cup rice
3½ cups hot chicken broth
½ teaspoon saffron
½ cup grated Parmesan

Sauté the onion and marrow in 4 tablespoons butter in a skillet for 3 minutes. Add rice, stir constantly for 1 or 2 minutes, and add 1 cup hot broth. Cook for 10 minutes, adding more broth as it is absorbed. Soak the saffron in 3 tablespoons water, and add the saffron and water with the remaining broth. Stir the rice with a fork, cover the pan, and continue to cook until the liquid is absorbed. Add the remaining butter and grated Parmesan cheese and stir well. SERVES 4.

Rice with Shrimps

RISOTTO CON SCAMPI

1½ pounds shrimps
½ cup (¼ pound) butter
1 tablespoon olive oil
1 onion, minced
2 cups rice
1 cup dry red wine
1 teaspoon chopped parsley
⅛ teaspoon marjoram

Boil shrimps in salted water to cover for 6 minutes or until they are done. Remove the shrimps and reserve 2 cups of the cooking liquid. Shell the shrimps and devein them. In a saucepan, melt the butter, add the olive oil, and cook the onion until it is golden. Add the rice and cook it for 1 minute, stirring, or until it is well coated with the butter. Add the wine; cook until it has evaporated and add the shrimp stock and seasoning. Cook for about 15 minutes longer or until the rice is done and the liquid is absorbed. Stir in the shrimps. SERVES 4.

FISH AND SHELLFISH

A glance at the map of Italy reveals why fish is so abundant in Italian markets: the country is almost entirely surrounded by water. Virtually every kind of fish has appeared on Italian tables from the time of the early Romans. Shellfish abound, from lobsters to tiny, brilliant prawns. Finger-shaped eels, sardines, squid: all can be had for the casting of a net. Mussels are a favorite, as are clams. And the fine Italian hand knows how to cook them all to their best advantage.

Baked Salmon with Lemon

SALMONE AL FORNO
CON LIMONE

4 small salmon steaks
4 tablespoons olive oil
1 teaspoon marjoram
1 clove garlic, minced
2 teaspoons minced onion
1 tablespoon chopped parsley
  Salt
  Pepper
3 tablespoons lemon juice
1 lemon, thinly sliced

Arrange the salmon in a shallow baking pan and add all
ingredients but lemon juice and lemon slices. Bake in a
moderately hot oven, 375° F., for 20 minutes; add lemon
juice and bake for 5 minutes longer, or until the salmon
is done. Turn once during baking. Arrange the fish on a
platter and garnish with lemon slices. SERVES 4.

Baked Swordfish Sicilian

PESCE SPADA AL FORNO

1 onion, chopped
3 tablespoons olive oil
1½ pounds swordfish
2½ cups (20-ounce can) tomatoes
½ cup dry white wine
Salt
Pepper
8 green olives, chopped
2 teaspoons marjoram
1 tablespoon capers
1 tablespoon chopped parsley
1 lemon, sliced

Brown onion in olive oil. Add tomatoes, wine, salt, and pepper and simmer, covered, for 15 minutes. Add olives, marjoram, capers, and parsley. Place fish in an oiled baking dish, pour the sauce over it, and bake in a moderately hot oven, 375° F., for 30 minutes, basting occasionally. Serve on a platter garnished with lemon slices. SERVES 4.

Lobster Fra Diavolo

ARAGOSTA ALLA FRA
DIAVOLO

4 lobsters
1 tablespoon olive oil
2 cloves garlic, minced
 Salt
 Pepper
1 onion, cut into rings
1 cup dry white wine
2½ cups (20-ounce can) tomatoes
 2 tablespoons tomato paste, mixed with 1
 tablespoon warm water
 2 tablespoons chopped parsley
 1 tablespoon orégano

Cut each lobster in 3 pieces and sauté the lobster in very hot olive oil for 4 minutes. Add garlic, salt, and pepper, and cook for 2 minutes more. Add onion rings. When the lobster turns red, add the wine and cook for 2 minutes longer. Add the tomatoes, tomato paste, parsley, and orégano. Cook over high heat for 8 minutes more. SERVES 4.

Mussels Steamed in Wine

ZUPPA DI COZZE

1 clove garlic
½ cup olive oil
2 tablespoons tomato paste, mixed with 1 cup
    warm water
¾ cup dry white wine
3 pounds mussels
2 teaspoons chopped parsley
½ teaspoon thyme
    Salt
    Pepper

Sauté garlic in olive oil in large saucepan until the garlic is golden. Discard the garlic; add the tomato paste and wine to the oil and cook over high heat for 10 minutes, or until the liquid is reduced to about three quarters of its original volume. Scrub the shells of the mussels well and add the mussels and seasoning. Cook over high heat, stirring occasionally, for 5 minutes or until all the mussel shells are open. SERVES 4.

Shrimp Marsala

SCAMPI AL MARSALA

2 pounds shrimp, shelled and deveined
½ cup flour
½ cup olive oil
½ cup dry Marsala wine
2 teaspoons tomato paste, mixed with 3
    tablespoons warm water
1 scallion, chopped
  Salt
  Pepper
2 teaspoons lemon juice

Dredge shrimp in flour and sauté in olive oil for 3 minutes. Drain the shrimp, reserving the oil. Add wine to shrimp and simmer for 5 minutes, or until shrimp is nearly done. Add reserved olive oil, tomato paste, scallion, salt, and pepper and simmer for 5 minutes longer or until shrimp is done. Stir in lemon juice. SERVES 4.

Piquant Baked Oysters

OSTRICHE PICCANTI

2 dozen oysters
1 clove garlic, split

   3 tablespoons butter
    Salt
    Pepper
   2 tablespoons olive oil
   1 tablespoon parsley
   1 cup bread crumbs
   1 teaspoon marjoram
    Juice of ½ lemon
   2 teaspoons chopped parsley
   1 lemon, cut into wedges

Scrub the shells well and rinse in cold water. Pry open the shells and remove the oysters. Rub the deep half-shells with the garlic and butter; put oysters back in the half-shells and sprinkle with salt and pepper. Mix all ingredients but lemon wedges, and top each oyster with some of the mixture. Arrange in a shallow baking pan and bake in a moderate oven, 350° F., for 10 minutes, or until edges of the oysters curl. Arrange on individual plates and garnish with lemon wedges. SERVES 4.

Seafood Stew

ZUPPA DI PESCE

Zuppa classifies this dish as a soup; actually, it is thick enough to come to table as a main-course stew. In Italy, squid and octopus frequently go into Zuppa di Pesce.

½ pound shrimp, shelled and deveined
1 pint mussels or Little Neck clams, in shell
1 pound cod, cut in chunks
2 pounds tomatoes, peeled and chopped
2 tablespoons chopped parsley
1 clove garlic, minced
  Salt
  Pepper
2 slices bread, cubed
2 tablespoons olive oil

Put all ingredients except bread and oil in a pan, add 2 tablespoons of water, and cook for 15 minutes, or until mussel shells open. Fry bread cubes in hot olive oil for 5 minutes, or until they are brown. Put the croutons in a bowl and add the stew. SERVES 4.

MEAT

Because meat is relatively scarce in Italy, the cook knows how to deal most effectively with each precious tidbit. What meat does reach the market, however, is excellent: the veal of Lombardy, the pork of Emilia and Romagna, the beef of Tuscany, the lamb that comes from the vicinity of Rome. Ham is popular; especially prosciutto, sliced thinly, and often combined with other foods. Italians enjoy variety meats; tripe, kidneys, brains and sweetbreads are favorites.

Veal Chops with Peppers

VITELLO CON PEPERONI

    4 green peppers, chopped
    1 onion, chopped
    4 tablespoons olive oil
    3 tablespoons chopped green olives
    1 tablespoon capers
1⅓ cups (11-ounce can) tomatoes
    2 anchovies, mashed
    1 clove garlic, minced
    4 loin veal chops
    2 tablespoons flour
    ½ cup broth or water

Fry peppers and onion in 1 tablespoon of olive oil for 5
minutes. Add olives, capers, and tomatoes. Cook for 20
minutes longer, or until peppers are very soft. In another pan heat anchovies and garlic in 1 tablespoon olive
oil until garlic is golden. Pour over pepper mixture and
keep it warm. Dredge chops lightly in flour and cook in
remaining olive oil for 20 minutes, or until the chops are
done. Remove chops to a platter. Pour broth into pan,
scraping in brown bits from pan bottom. Cook for 3 minutes, and pour sauce over chops. Surround the chops with
the pepper mixture. SERVES 4.

Breaded Veal Cutlets

COTOLETTE ALLA

MILANESE

8 veal cutlets, pounded thin
   Salt
   Pepper
2 eggs, beaten
1 cup bread crumbs
½ cup (¼ pound) butter

Sprinkle cutlets with salt and pepper, dip them in beaten eggs, and roll them in bread crumbs. Sauté the cutlets in butter until they are golden. SERVES 4.

Veal Scaloppine with Chicken Livers

SCALOPPINE ALLA

BUONGUSTAIA

¼ cup flour
   Salt
   Pepper
8 veal cutlets, pounded thin
½ teaspoon sage
3 tablespoons butter
6 chicken livers, chopped
1 tomato, peeled and chopped

Season flour with salt and pepper. Dip cutlets in it, sprinkle them with sage, and brown lightly in butter. Add chicken livers; sauté them for 3 minutes and add the tomato. Cook for 5 minutes longer. Serve the veal on a platter with the chicken-liver sauce. SERVES 4.

Veal Scaloppine Marsala

SCALOPPINE DI VITELLO
AL MARSALA

8 veal cutlets, pounded thin
1 teaspoon lemon juice
¼ cup flour
  Salt
  Pepper
6 tablespoons butter
½ cup dry Marsala wine
1 lemon, thinly sliced

Sprinkle veal cutlets with lemon juice. Season flour with salt and pepper and roll the veal in it. Sauté veal in butter for 3 minutes on each side. Add Marsala wine and simmer for 2 minutes more. Arrange the veal on a platter, pour the pan juices over it, and garnish with lemon slices. SERVES 4.

Veal Scaloppine Parmesan

SCALOPPINE ALLA

PARMIGIANA

8 veal cutlets
Salt
Pepper
1 teaspoon orégano
5 tablespoons grated Parmesan cheese
3 tablespoons olive oil
1 lemon, thinly sliced

Sprinkle the cutlets with salt, pepper, and orégano, and coat evenly with cheese. Sauté the meat in olive oil for about 6 minutes, or until it is done. Garnish the veal with lemon slices. SERVES 4.

Veal Scaloppine with Prosciutto

SALTIMBOCCA

"Saltimbocca" means literally "jump into the mouth." As any Roman will confirm, the dish is so delicious it jumps off the table and into the diner's mouth in its eagerness for praise.

8 slices prosciutto or boiled ham
8 veal cutlets, pounded thin
1 teaspoon sage
  Salt
  Pepper
3 tablespoons butter

Lay a slice of prosciutto on each cutlet and sprinkle with sage, salt, and pepper. Do not roll up, but secure meat slices flat with toothpicks. Sauté the meat in butter for 3 minutes on each side. Discard toothpicks. Serve on toast or on a bed of chopped spinach and garnish with slices of hard-cooked egg, if desired. SERVES 4.

Veal Scaloppine with Prosciutto and Cheese

BOCCONCINI

Proceed as for Saltimbocca (above), using the same ingredients, but add a few slivers of Gruyère cheese between the veal and prosciutto. SERVES 4.

Veal Stew with Peas

SPEZZATO DI VITELLO
CON PISELLI

1 onion, minced
4 tablespoons butter
1½ pounds stewing veal, cut in 1-inch pieces
½ cup dry white wine
1 cup beef or chicken broth
1 clove garlic, minced
Salt
Pepper
1½ pounds peas
2 teaspoons chopped parsley

Sauté onion in butter until it is golden. Add meat and brown it on all sides. Add wine and cook over high heat until wine has evaporated. Add broth, garlic, salt, and pepper; simmer, covered, for 1 hour, adding more broth if necessary. Add peas and parsley and simmer stew for 10 minutes longer, or until peas are tender. SERVES 4.

Veal Stuffed with Pork

VITELLO RIPIENO

1½ slices white bread
⅓ cup milk
½ pound ground pork
6 tablespoons grated Parmesan cheese
¼ teaspoon nutmeg
1½ tablespoons chopped parsley
2 eggs, well beaten
Salt
Pepper
4-pound shoulder of veal, boned
5 slices bacon
2 cloves garlic
3 tablespoons olive oil

Soak bread in milk for 5 minutes, or until it is soaked through, and then squeeze the bread dry. Mix the bread well with the pork, cheese, nutmeg, parsley, eggs, salt, and pepper. Stuff the veal with the mixture, roll the meat, and cover it with bacon strips. Secure the roll with string. Fry the garlic in oil until it is golden; discard the garlic. Add the veal to the pan and sear over high heat for 10 minutes, turning frequently. Reduce the heat and cook the veal for 1 hour. Add wine and simmer the meat for 45 minutes longer, or until it is done. SERVES 8.

Marrowbones Milanese

OSSO BUCO

    2 pounds veal shank, cut in 2-inch pieces
    ¼ cup flour
    3 tablespoons butter
    ½ cup dry white wine
    2 tomatoes, peeled and chopped
    1 onion, chopped
    1 carrot, sliced
    1 cup beef broth or water
    1 clove garlic, minced
      Salt
      Pepper
      Grated peel of ½ lemon
    2 tablespoons chopped parsley

Dredge the shank pieces in flour, brown in butter, and add
wine. Simmer for 10 minutes. Add tomatoes, onion, carrot, broth, garlic, salt, and pepper. Cook the bones,
covered, for 1½ hours, adding more liquid if necessary
and skimming from time to time. Add lemon peel and
parsley and simmer for 5 minutes longer. Serve with
Risotto alla Milanese (see index). SERVES 4.

Mixed Fry

FRITTO MISTO

This dish allows the cook the fun of improvisation. Mixed Fry is composed of bits of meat and vegetable, dipped in batter, deep fried, and served on a large platter. The following list may serve as an ingredients guide; you can combine meats and vegetables as taste dictates.

> Chicken breast, fileted
> Veal cutlets, pounded thin
> Calf's liver
> Sweetbreads, parboiled
> Calf's brain, parboiled
> Artichoke hearts, parboiled and halved
> Cauliflower flowerets, parboiled
> Zucchini, thinly sliced
> Eggplant, thinly sliced

Each piece should be bite-sized. Season the pieces with salt and pepper, dip in frying batter, and fry in deep hot oil, 370° F. The veal, chicken, and artichokes should go in first; they take longest to cook, about 5 minutes. Add the other ingredients and fry until all are golden brown. Drain the Fritto Misto on absorbent paper and serve it immediately on a hot platter garnished with lemon wedges.

Frying Batter

1 cup flour
3 tablespoons olive oil
  Salt
1 egg white, beaten

Blend flour with olive oil and add salt. Gradually stir in
¾ cup lukewarm water; mix batter. It should be the consistency of light cream. Let the batter stand for 1 hour,
stir in egg white.

Fillet of Beef with Eggplant

MEDAGLIONI ALLA
ARLESIANA

4 slices peeled eggplant, ½ inch thick
¼ cup flour
1 egg, beaten
1 cup olive oil
1 clove garlic
4 slices fillet of beef
4 slices Mozzarella cheese
  Salt
  Pepper
1 teaspoon chopped parsley
  Fried onion rings

Dip eggplant slices in flour, then in egg, then in flour again. Fry in oil for 8 minutes, or until cooked through. Remove eggplant, drain on absorbent paper. Pour off all but 3 tablespoons oil from the pan. Sauté the garlic for 5 minutes and then discard. Add beef and sauté for 5 minutes or until done, depending on the thickness of the meat; it should be rare. Arrange the meat on an ovenproof platter and place a slice of eggplant and a slice of Mozzarella on each fillet. Sprinkle with salt, pepper, and parsley. Place in a hot oven, 400° F., for 3 minutes, or until the cheese is melted. Garnish the platter with the onion rings. SERVES 4.

Beef Stuffed with Ham

MANZO RIPIENO
DI PROSCIUTTO

1 onion, chopped
½ carrot, chopped
1 tablespoon chopped parsley
2 chicken livers, chopped
2 slices white bread, soaked in water and
      pressed dry
1 cup prosciutto or boiled ham, cut in
      julienne
2 tablespoons grated Parmesan cheese
1 egg, beaten
1 teaspoon orégano

Salt

Pepper

1½-pound slice rump or shoulder of beef

   3 tablespoons olive oil

   1 cup dry red wine

Mix well the onion, carrot, parsley, chicken livers, bread, ham, cheese, egg, and seasonings. Pound the beef with a knife handle and spread it with the stuffing. Roll up the beef, tie it with string, and brown it in olive oil. Add 1 cup red wine and roast the meat in a slow oven, 325° F., for 2 hours, or until it is done. Serve in slices. Manzo Ripieno di Prosciutto may also be served cold. SERVES 4.

Roast Beef with Onions

ARROSTO DI MANZO
ALLA LIVORNESE

   2 strips bacon

   4-pound top round of beef

   8 whole cloves

   2 cups dry red wine

   2 tablespoons chopped parsley

   1 clove garlic

     Salt

     Pepper

   6 small white onions, parboiled

   2 tablespoons butter

Chop the bacon in coarse pieces, make incisions in the roast, and insert pieces of bacon. Press cloves into roast. Place meat in a bowl with wine, parsley, garlic, salt, and pepper and let it marinate overnight. Drain the meat, pat it dry, and place it in a roasting pan with onions. Spread butter on meat and roast it in a moderate oven, 350° F., for 1¼ hours for rare, or until it is done to your taste. Skim frequently and add some marinade to the pan juices from time to time for basting. Strain the remaining marinade, heat it, and add it to the pan juices. Slice the roast and serve with pan juices. SERVES 8.

Savory Pot Roast

MANZO ALLA LOMBARDA

3 slices bacon, minced
3-pound top round of beef
1 carrot, sliced
1 stalk celery, chopped
1 onion, chopped
2 tablespoons chopped parsley
2-inch strip lemon peel, grated
½ cup dry red wine
½ cup beef broth or water
1 teaspoon orégano
  Salt
  Pepper

Cook bacon in heavy casserole until it is golden; add meat and brown it. Add remaining ingredients and simmer, covered, for 3 hours, or until meat is tender, skimming occasionally. Add more broth or water if necessary. Remove the meat to a platter and add the vegetables and sauce. SERVES 6.

Steak Florentine

BISTECCA ALLA FIORENTINA

3 pounds sirloin or porterhouse steak
½ cup olive oil
  Salt
  Pepper
2 teaspoons lemon juice
2 tablespoons butter

Combine the olive oil with the salt, pepper, and lemon juice. Rub the steak with the mixture, and then let the steak marinate for 2 hours. Drain the steak and broil it under high heat for 5 minutes on each side for rare or until it is done to your taste, depending on thickness. Add butter and serve. SERVES 4.

Meat Balls Stuffed with Almonds

POLPETTINE CON
SORPRESE

This is a meat ball "surprise." The *polpettine* may be stuffed with small chunks of cooked Italian sausage, salami, or leftover meat instead of almonds.

    1 pound ground beef
    2 eggs, beaten
    ½ cup bread crumbs
    3 tablespoons milk
      Salt
      Pepper
    1 tablespoon chopped parsley
      Almonds as needed
    2 tablespoons butter

Mix well the meat, eggs, 2 tablespoons bread crumbs, milk, and seasoning. Shape the mixture into little meat balls around the almonds, roll them in remaining bread crumbs, and fry them in butter for 8 minutes, or until they are done. SERVES 4.

Meat Balls with Sausage

POLPETTINE DI MANZO
E SALSICCIA

1 pound sweet Italian sausages
1 pound ground beef
1 clove garlic, minced
1 tablespoon chopped parsley
6 slices white bread, soaked in milk and
    pressed dry
2 eggs, beaten
 Salt
 Pepper
1 cup dry bread crumbs
¾ cup olive oil

Remove the sausage meat from casing and mix with beef, garlic, parsley, soaked bread crumbs, eggs, salt, and pepper. Shape into meat balls about 2 inches in diameter, roll in dry bread crumbs, and fry a few at a time in hot oil for 10 minutes, or until meat balls are brown. SERVES 6.

64

MEAT

Calf's Liver with Onions

FEGATO DI VITELLO
ALLA VENEZIANA

2 large onions, sliced
2 tablespoons olive oil
2 tablespoons butter
1¼ pound calf's liver, sliced small
Salt
Pepper

Sauté the onion in olive oil and butter until it is golden;
add the liver and salt and pepper. Cook over medium-
high heat for about 6 minutes, or until the liver is done.
(Do not overcook the liver; it should be slightly pink in-
side.) SERVES 4.

Calf's Liver with Wine Sauce

FEGATO DI VITELLO
AL VINO

2 tablespoons minced onion
1 clove garlic
1 tablespoon chopped parsley

   4 tablespoons olive oil
1¼ pounds calf's liver, thinly sliced
   ½ cup dry white wine
   ¼ cup broth or water
   3 tablespoons bread crumbs
      Salt
      Pepper
   2 tablespoons grated Parmesan cheese

Sauté onion, garlic, and parsley in olive oil until onion is soft. Discard garlic. Add liver, wine, and broth. Sprinkle bread crumbs over the mixture and cook for 8 minutes, or until liver is done. Remove liver and cook sauce for 5 minutes more. Add salt and pepper. Return liver to pan; sprinkle with cheese and simmer for 1 minute more. SERVES 4.

Roast Lamb with Zucchini

AGNELLO E ZUCCHINI

   5-pound leg of lamb
      Salt
      Pepper
1½ teaspoon crushed rosemary
   1 clove garlic, slivered
   2 tablespoons butter, softened
   ½ cup olive oil

4 small zucchini, split lengthwise in quarters
2 teaspoons basil
¾ cup dry red wine

Rub lamb with salt, pepper, and rosemary; make incisions in the meat and insert slivers of garlic. Rub the meat with softened butter; pour the olive oil over the meat, and heat in a hot oven, 400° F., for 10 minutes. Reduce the heat to 325° F.; sprinkle the zucchini with basil and add it and the wine to the meat. Roast the lamb for 2¼ hours, or until it is done. Baste every 15 minutes with the red wine, adding more wine if necessary. SERVES 8.

Intoxicated Pork

MAIALE UBRIACATO

5 pounds loin of pork
1 clove garlic, split
Salt
Pepper
1 cup Chianti wine
½ cup tomato paste, mixed with 1 cup water
2 tablespoons chopped parsley

Rub pork with garlic, salt, and pepper. Brown the meat in its own fat. Add wine and simmer, covered, until wine has evaporated, turning meat occasionally. Add the tomato paste and parsley, and simmer, covered, for 2½ hours, or until meat is well done, turning occasionally and skimming from time to time. Transfer meat to a platter and pour sauce over it. SERVES 8.

Pork Chops Florentine

COSTOLETTE DI MAIALE
ALLA FIORENTINA

1 clove garlic, minced
1 tablespoon olive oil
8 thin pork chops
½ cup dry red wine
Salt
Pepper

Fry garlic in olive oil until it is golden. Add chops and fry until brown. Add wine, salt, and pepper, and cook over low heat until wine is reduced to ½ its original quantity and the chops are well cooked. Remove chops and serve. SERVES 4.

POULTRY

As in America, Italians serve chicken to add cheer to festive occasions. In Tuscany, where the best Italian chickens are raised, tender young chickens are most often grilled; in Bologna, chicken breasts are sautéed in butter; in Rome, chicken goes into the casserole with rice and vegetables. Italians dote on any winged creature. A stroll through the markets reveals all kinds of birds for the pot, from huge turkeys to tiny larks.

Chicken Breasts with Cheese

PETTI DI POLLO ALLA
BOLOGNESE

Salt
Pepper
1 egg, beaten
Breasts of two 3-pound broiler-fryers, each
     halved, boned, and pounded thin
4 tablespoons flour
4 tablespoons butter
2 tablespoons Marsala wine
4 tablespoons grated Parmesan cheese
4 slices prosciutto
4 thin slices Mozzarella cheese

Add salt and pepper to the beaten egg. Dip the chicken
breasts into the egg and then dip them lightly in flour.
Brown the chicken in butter on both sides over high heat
and stir in the wine. Spread 1 tablespoon grated Parmesan
cheese over each fillet. Reduce the heat, cover the pan, and
sauté for 5 minutes longer, or until the cheese is melted.
Arrange over each fillet a slice of prosciutto, cut the same
size as the chicken breast, and a slice of Mozzarella cheese.
Place in moderately hot oven, 375° F., for 10 minutes.
SERVES 4.

Creamed Chicken Breasts

CREMA DI PETTI DI POLLO

Breasts of two 3-pound broiler-fryers,
    each halved, boned, and pounded thin
1 egg yolk, beaten
4 tablespoons flour
4 tablespoons butter
5 tablespoons tomato sauce
6 tablespoons heavy cream
  Juice of ½ lemon
  Salt
  Pepper
2 slices bread, toasted and cubed
1 tablespoon chopped parsley

Dip the chicken in egg yolk and then in flour. Sauté the meat in butter until it is golden. Add tomato sauce, cream, lemon juice, salt, and pepper and simmer for 20 minutes, or until the chicken is done, stirring frequently. Be careful not to let the sauce come to a boil. Place the chicken on a hot serving platter and pour the sauce over it. Cover with croutons and sprinkle with parsley. SERVES 4.

Chicken Cacciatora

SPEZZATINO DI POLLO

ALLA CACCIATORA

3½ pound broiler-fryer, cut into serving pieces
½ cup flour
½ cup olive oil
1 small onion, chopped
1 clove garlic, minced
1 carrot, chopped
1 tablespoon chopped parsley
1 bay leaf, crushed
3 cups canned Italian tomatoes
   Pepper
3 anchovies, mashed
1 cup Chianti wine

Dredge chicken in flour and brown in olive oil in a skillet. Remove the chicken and in the remaining oil sauté onion, garlic, carrot, parsley, and bay leaf until the onion is golden. Strain the tomatoes and add the tomato pulp to the skillet. Add pepper and anchovies. Bring the sauce to a boil. Add the chicken and Chianti and simmer for 45 minutes, or until the chicken is tender. SERVES 4.

Chicken Marengo

POLLO ALLA MARENGO

This delectable dish is a favorite both in France and in Italy. It was first concocted by the chef of Napoleon at the Battle of Marengo.

3½-pound broiler-fryer, cut into serving pieces
    Salt
    Pepper
¼ teaspoon nutmeg
6 tablespoons butter
2 tablespoons olive oil
1 tablespoon flour
    Juice of 1 lemon
1 cup dry white wine
    Parsley sprigs

Sprinkle chicken with salt, pepper, and nutmeg, and brown in butter and olive oil for 20 minutes. Remove the chicken from the pan and add the flour, lemon juice, and wine, stirring well to blend. Return the chicken to the pan and cook over low heat for 30 more minutes. Remove the chicken to a platter, pour the sauce over it, and garnish the platter with sprigs of parsley. SERVES 4.

Chicken Tetrazzini

SPAGHETTI ALLA
TETRAZZINI

3-pound broiler-fryer, cut into serving pieces
½ pound mushrooms, sliced
6 tablespoons butter
½ pound spaghetti, broken
2 tablespoons flour
1 cup cream
  Sherry to taste
¼ teaspoon nutmeg
  Salt
  Pepper
½ cup grated Parmesan cheese

Poach chicken in salted water for 40 minutes, or until it is tender. Remove the meat from the bones and cut it into strips. Reserve 2 cups of the broth. Sauté the mushrooms in 2 tablespoons butter. Cook the spaghetti until it is almost done but still firm. Melt 3 tablespoons butter, stir in the flour, and add the cream. Cook the cream sauce over low heat, stirring frequently, until it is thick. Add 2 cups reserved chicken broth, the sherry, and seasonings. Place the spaghetti, chicken, and sauce in a buttered casserole and mix well. Sprinkle with grated cheese, dot with the remaining butter, and bake in a moderate oven, 350° F., for 30 minutes. SERVES 4.

Fried Lemon Chicken

POLLO AL LIMONE

2 cups olive oil
4 tablespoons lemon juice
  Salt
  Pepper
2 teaspoons chopped parsley
3½-pound broiler-fryer, cut into serving pieces
1 egg, beaten
1½ cups flour
1 lemon, thinly sliced

Combine ½ cup olive oil, lemon juice, salt, pepper, and parsley and brush the chicken with the marinade. Marinate for 3 hours, brushing the chicken with the liquid from time to time. Dry the chicken, dip it into the beaten egg and then into the flour. Fry the chicken in the remaining olive oil for 15 to 20 minutes on each side, or until it is done. Drain on paper towels. Serve the chicken on a platter garnished with the lemon slices. SERVES 4.

Chicken with Ham

POLLO ALLA ROMANA

 3-pound broiler-fryer, cut into serving pieces
 4 tablespoons olive oil
 ⅓ pound prosciutto, cut in small pieces
   Salt
   Pepper
 1 clove garlic, minced
 1 teaspoon marjoram
 ⅔ cup dry red wine
 2½ cups (20-ounce can) Italian tomatoes

Cook the chicken in hot oil with prosciutto, salt, and pepper until the chicken is golden. Add minced garlic, marjoram, and wine, and simmer until the wine has evaporated. Add the tomatoes and cook for 40 minutes more, or until the chicken is done. There should be a small amount of dark, thick sauce. SERVES 4.

Duck in Wine

ANITRA AL VINO

1 clove garlic, split
4 tablespoons olive oil
4-pound duck, cut into serving pieces
1 tablespoon chopped parsley
1 teaspoon poultry seasoning
½ teaspoon thyme
  Salt
  Pepper
2 cups (16-ounce can) Italian tomatoes,
    chopped
1 cup dry white wine
½ pound mushrooms, sliced
10 green olives, sliced

Sauté the garlic in olive oil until it is golden and discard
the garlic. Brown the duck in the oil over high heat for
10 minutes, stirring occasionally. Add the seasonings and
tomatoes, reduce the heat, and simmer, covered, for 30
minutes, skimming from time to time. Add the wine and
continue to simmer the duck, uncovered, for 30 minutes
longer. Add mushrooms and olives and simmer for 30
minutes more, stirring occasionally. Skim well before
serving. SERVES 4.

Roast Turkey with Chestnut Dressing

TACCHINO ARROSTO

RIPIENO DI CASTAGNE

1 pound chestnuts
2 cups (1 pound) butter, melted
  Salt
  Pepper
1 egg
4 slices salami, diced
2 cups bread crumbs
1 teaspoon marjoram
1 small onion, chopped
1 turkey liver, minced
  Juice of 1 lemon
12- to 14-pound turkey
2 cups Chianti wine

Cut slits in the chestnuts, boil them for 15 minutes, and
let them cool. Remove the shells and skins and boil the
chestnuts in salted water for 15 minutes longer, or until
they are just soft. Drain the chestnuts, chop them, and
mash them. Combine them with 3 tablespoons melted butter and all other ingredients except remaining butter and
Chianti. Stuff the turkey with the dressing, secure the open-
ing, and truss the bird. Place in a roasting pan, brush with
remaining butter, and roast in a moderate oven, 325° F.,
for 5 hours or until done, basting frequently. When it
has cooked 2½ hours, add wine. SERVES 10 TO 12.

VEGETABLES

Italians think too highly of vegetables to let them merely "come with" the main course. They shine on their own, either as a separate course or as an important adjunct to the meat, poultry, or fish. Plain, limp boiled vegetables would cause a gastronomic scandal in Italy. Vegetables go into a variety of sauces and marinades, or, if simply cooked, are accompanied by butter and grated cheese or lemon juice to give added zest. Dried beans play an important role in salads, with pasta, or combined with other vegetables and meats. Peas and squashes (especially small, sweet zucchini) play an important role in the vegetable repertory, as well as all kinds of greens: dandelion leaves, lettuces, fennel, and others often overlooked by the American cook.

Artichokes Stuffed with Cheese

CARCIOFI ALLA

PARMIGIANA

4 artichokes
1 cup bread crumbs
1 cup grated Parmesan cheese
1 tablespoon chopped parsley
  Salt
  Pepper
4 cloves garlic, split
½ cup olive oil

Cut the stems of the artichokes and with scissors trim ½ inch from the tip of each leaf. Parboil the artichokes for 5 minutes in boiling salted water; drain them and press the artichokes, top down, against a plate to loosen the leaves. Mix together well the bread crumbs, grated cheese, parsley, salt, and pepper. Spoon a little stuffing into the base of each leaf. Place a garlic clove in the center of each artichoke, put them in a casserole, and add water ½ inch deep. Pour about 2 tablespoons olive oil over each artichoke, cover the casserole, and bake in a slow oven, 300° F., for 45 minutes, or until the artichokes are done. Discard the garlic cloves before serving. The stuffed artichokes may also be chilled and served cold. SERVES 4.

Asparagus Parmesan

ASPARAGI ALLA
PARMIGIANA

2 pounds asparagus
4 tablespoons melted butter
  Salt
  Pepper
2 tablespoons grated Parmesan cheese
¼ pound Mozzarella cheese, cut into slivers

Cook asparagus in 1 cup water, covered, for 12 minutes, or until it is almost done. Place it in a baking dish, pour butter over it, and add salt, pepper, Mozzarella slivers, and grated Parmesan cheese. Bake in a hot oven, 400° F., for 10 minutes, or until grated cheese is brown. SERVES 4.

Beans with Garlic

FAGIOLI ALL'UCCELLETTO

In Florence, as throughout the rest of Tuscany, white beans are eaten frequently and with great gusto.

¾ pound white beans
2 cloves garlic, each split
2 tablespoons olive oil
½ teaspoon sage
    Salt
    Pepper
2 teaspoons tomato paste

Soak the beans overnight in water to cover. Boil the beans in 1 quart water for 1½ hours and drain them. Sauté the garlic in the olive oil until it is golden. Discard the garlic and add the beans to the oil in the pan with sage, salt, pepper, and tomato paste. Simmer, stirring, for 20 minutes. SERVES 4.

Broccoli with Olives

BROCCOLI CON OLIVE

1 onion, sliced
8 black olives, chopped
2 anchovies, chopped
4 tablespoons olive oil
1 bunch broccoli, thinly sliced
½ cup grated Parmesan cheese
   Pepper
1 cup dry red wine

Combine onion, olives, and anchovies. Pour 1 tablespoon olive oil in the bottom of a large saucepan and add a layer of the olive mixture, a layer of broccoli, and a layer of grated cheese. Sprinkle with pepper and olive oil. Continue this process until all these ingredients are used, ending with a sprinkling of olive oil. Add wine and cook over low heat for 30 minutes, or until broccoli is tender. Do not stir. SERVES 4.

Cabbage with Wine

CAVOLI CON VINO

This delicious cabbage dish goes especially well with roast pork.

    1 white cabbage, shredded
    1 onion, chopped
    2 tablespoons olive oil
    1 cup chopped tomatoes
    2 teaspoons fennel seeds
      Salt
      Pepper
    ½ cup dry white wine
    ¼ teaspoon lemon juice
    3 tablespoons grated Parmesan cheese

Sauté cabbage and onion in olive oil for 10 minutes. Add tomato, fennel seeds, salt, and pepper. Cook, covered, for 15 minutes longer. Add wine and lemon juice and cook for 10 minutes more, or until the cabbage is tender. Sprinkle with grated cheese. SERVES 4.

Celery Parmesan

SEDANI ALLA PARMIGIANA

2 bunches celery, cut in ½-inch slices
4 tablespoons butter
½ cup chicken broth
  Salt
  Pepper
½ cup grated Parmesan cheese

Sauté celery in butter for 5 minutes, stirring frequently.
Add broth, salt, and pepper and simmer, covered, for 15
minutes. Drain the celery, being careful not to break up
the pieces. Arrange in a buttered baking dish and sprinkle
with cheese. Bake in a hot oven, 425° F., for 10 minutes,
or until the top is brown. SERVES 4.

Fried Eggplant

MELANZANE FRITTE

2 eggs
  Salt
  Pepper
2 small eggplants, peeled and sliced very
      thin
1 cup bread crumbs
2 cups olive oil

Beat the eggs with salt and pepper. Roll the eggplant slices
in the crumbs, then in the eggs, then in the crumbs again.
Let the eggplant slices dry and fry them in a basket in
deep, hot olive oil until brown. SERVES 4.

Eggplant with Cheese

MELANZANE ALLA

PARMIGIANA

    Fried Eggplant (see recipe above)
1 clove garlic
3 tablespoons olive oil
2 pounds Italian plum tomatoes, chopped
½ teaspoon basil
    Salt
    Pepper
1 cup grated Parmesan cheese
¼ pound Mozzarella cheese, cut into slivers
2 tablespoons butter

Make Fried Eggplant according to recipe directions above.
Sauté garlic in olive oil until the garlic is golden. Add
tomatoes, basil, salt, and pepper; and cook for 20 minutes.
In a casserole, arrange a layer of the eggplant, a layer of
tomato sauce, and a layer of each cheese. Dot with butter.
Continue to make layers and dot with butter in this fashion
until all the ingredients are used. Bake the casserole in a
moderate oven, 350° F., for 30 minutes. SERVES 4.

Mushrooms with Pine Nuts

FUNGHI CON PINOLI

1 pound mushrooms, sliced
3 tablespoons butter
  Salt
  Pepper
½ onion, chopped
½ cup pine nuts
3 tablespoons dry white wine

Cook the mushrooms in butter for 3 minutes. Add remaining ingredients, and cook for 5 minutes longer, or until the mushrooms are done and the nuts are golden. SERVES 4.

Peas with Onion and Bacon

PISELLI ALLA ROMANA

2 slices bacon, diced
1 pound peas
1 small onion, chopped
3 tablespoons butter
  Salt
  Pepper

Simmer bacon in 3 tablespoons water for 5 minutes, add peas and onion, and cook over low heat for 15 minutes. Remove the peas to a serving dish, add the butter and salt and pepper. If desired, garnish with croutons. SERVES 4.

Fried Peppers

PEPERONI FRITTI

6 green peppers, coarsely chopped
5 tablespoons olive oil
1 clove garlic, split
  Salt
  Pepper

Parboil peppers for 3 minutes, drain, and dry on absorbent paper. Brown the peppers over high heat in olive oil with garlic for 5 minutes, stirring occasionally. Reduce the heat and cook, covered, for 10 minutes, or until the peppers are soft. Discard garlic. Sprinkle with salt and pepper. Serve with veal or Italian sausage. Fried Peppers may also be chilled and served on the Antipasto platter. SERVES 4.

Potato Tart with Cheese

TORTA DI PATATE
AL FORMAGGIO

3 potatoes, boiled and mashed
1 cup flour
 Salt
 Pepper
4 tablespoons olive oil
½ cup canned tomatoes, drained
¼ pound Mozzarella cheese, diced
2 tablespoons grated Parmesan cheese
2 teaspoons marjoram
1 teaspoon basil

To the mashed potatoes add flour, salt, and pepper and mix well. Oil the bottom of a large shallow baking dish and spread the potato mixture ½ inch thick on the bottom. Sprinkle well with 2 tablespoons olive oil. Add tomatoes, cheeses, marjoram, basil, salt and pepper. Sprinkle with remaining olive oil and bake in a hot oven, 400° F., for 30 minutes, or until cheese is brown. SERVES 4.

Spinach with Pine Nuts

SPINACI CON PINOLI

1½ pounds spinach
3 tablespoons olive oil
 Salt
 Pepper
1½ tablespoons raisins
1½ tablespoons shelled pine nuts
 ½ cup (¼ pound) butter

Cook the spinach in 1 cup water for 5 minutes; drain, add olive oil, and cook over low heat for 5 minutes longer. Plump raisins in hot water for 2 minutes. Add raisins, pine nuts, and butter to the spinach. SERVES 4.

Zucchini Casserole

ZUCCHINI AL FORNO

1 red Italian onion, cut into rings
 Pepper
3 tablespoons butter
2 cups thinly sliced zucchini
2 tomatoes, peeled and cut into wedges
 Salt
¼ cup grated Parmesan cheese

Sauté the onion rings and pepper in the butter until the onion is golden. Add the zucchini and sauté for 5 minutes more. Add the tomato wedges and sauté for 5 minutes longer. Add salt and pepper. Turn the vegetables into a casserole and sprinkle with grated cheese. Bake the casserole in a moderately hot oven, 375° F., for 10 minutes, or until the topping is brown. SERVES 4.

Anchovy Sauce for Vegetables

BAGNA CAUDA

Bagna cauda literally means "hot bath." The classical Piedmont version calls for a sliced truffle and a much larger quantity of garlic. The "hot bath" is used as a dip for artichokes, scallions, strips of pepper or celery or other raw vegetables.

1 can anchovies
2 cloves garlic, minced
½ cup olive oil
½ cup (¼ pound) butter

Drain the anchovies, reserving the oil, and mash them. Cook for 10 minutes with garlic in olive oil, butter, and reserved anchovy oil, stirring constantly. Serve very hot.

Fennel Salad

INSALATA DI FINOCCHI

2 bunches fennel
½ cup olive oil
2 tablespoons wine vinegar
Salt
Freshly ground black pepper

Separate the chilled fennel stalks and slice them. Combine
the remaining ingredients to make a dressing and pour it
over the fennel. SERVES 4.

Garden Salad

INSALATA AL BOSCO

2 large potatoes, boiled in their jackets and
      diced
2 cups green beans, cooked
1 clove garlic, split
⅓ cup olive oil
2 tablespoons wine vinegar
Salt
Pepper
4 hard-cooked eggs
8 slices ham

    2 tomatoes
    Mayonnaise
    2 tablespoons lemon juice

Combine potatoes, green beans, garlic, oil, vinegar, salt, and pepper and toss well. Marinate the vegetables in the refrigerator for 3 hours. Discard the garlic and arrange the vegetables on a platter. Halve the eggs, roll each half in a ham slice, and arrange them around the border of a platter. Halve the tomatoes and place them, cut side down, on the vegetables. Dot with mayonnaise and sprinkle with lemon juice. SERVES 4.

Shrimp and Rice Salad

INSALATA DI RISOTTO
E SCAMPI

  2½ cups chicken broth
    1 cup rice
    ½ pound shrimps, cooked, shelled, and
        deveined
    2 tablespoons olive oil
    1 teaspoon wine vinegar
    Salt
    Pepper
    2 tablespoons chopped parsley
    ½ cucumber, sliced

Bring the broth to a boil, add the rice, and simmer, covered, for 25 minutes, or until all the liquid is absorbed. Add all ingredients but the cucumber; chill and serve on lettuce leaves. Garnish with the cucumber slices. SERVES 4.

DESSERTS

If the meal has been hearty, Italians generally choose to top it off with fruit and cheese rather than a sweet. Italian cheeses are excellent, and range from mild Bel Paese to sharp Gorgonzola. Pastries and desserts generally make their appearance later in the evening, when guests drop in, or at the end of a formal dinner. Fluffy zabaglione is a favorite, as are crisp amaretti (little macaroons) and fruitcake. One of the simplest and best Italian desserts is sliced fruit, chilled and marinated in wine. Ice cream is a favorite, and ices have been popular since ancient Roman times.

Baked Apples with Raisins

MELA COTTA CON

UVA PASSA

¾ cup raisins
1¼ cups white wine
8 greening apples
½ teaspoon grated lemon rind
4 tablespoons sugar
¾ teaspoon cinnamon
½ teaspoon nutmeg
2 tablespoons butter
1 cup cream

Plump raisins in wine for 5 minutes, drain, and reserve the wine. Core apples and stuff centers with raisins. Sprinkle with grated lemon rind, sugar, cinnamon, and nutmeg. Dot the apples with butter and pour the reserved wine over them. Bake in a moderately hot oven, 375° F., for 45 minutes, or until the apples are soft. Serve hot or cold with cream. SERVES 8.

Chestnuts with Marsala

CASTAGNE AL MARSALA

1 pound chestnuts
1½ cups Marsala wine
½ cup Port wine
3 tablespoons sugar
½ cup cream, whipped

Score the chestnuts across the rounded sides with a sharp paring knife, and boil them in water to cover for 10 minutes. Let them cool slightly and peel them. Put them in a saucepan, add the wines and sugar, and simmer until the chestnuts are cooked through and the wine is syrupy. Serve hot or cold with the wine syrup and whipped cream. SERVES 4.

Oranges in Wine

ARANCE AL VINO

4 oranges
1 tablespoon sugar
2 cups dry white wine
Cinnamon stick
¼ teaspoon nutmeg
3 whole cloves

Peel the oranges, cut them into thin slices, and sprinkle them with sugar. Cover the slices with the wine, add the spices, and chill in the refrigerator for 6 hours. SERVES 4.

Peaches Stuffed with Almonds

PESCHE IMBOTTITE

ALLA MANDORLA

4 large peaches
4 tablespoons minced toasted almonds
3 tablespoons powdered sugar
2 teaspoons chopped glazed lemon peel
1 teaspoon cinnamon
6 tablespoons dry white wine

Peel, pit, and halve the peaches. Mix the almonds with 1½ tablespoons powdered sugar and the chopped lemon peel. Fill the peach halves with the mixture, sprinkle with the remaining sugar and the cinnamon, and pour the wine over them. Bake in a moderate oven, 350° F., for 10 minutes. SERVES 4.

Strawberry Ice

GRANITA DI FRAGOLA

1 quart fresh strawberries
Juice of ½ lemon
Juice of 2 oranges
2½ cups sugar

Wash and hull the berries and then put them through a sieve. Add the lemon juice and orange juice. Put the sugar and ½ cup water in a saucepan and cook for 5 minutes. Allow the sugar syrup to cool and add it to the strawberry mixture. Pour the mixture into a refrigerator tray and let it freeze until firm, stirring well from time to time to prevent ice crystals from forming. Serve with cookies. SERVES 6.

Ricotta Cheese Pie

TORTA DI RICOTTA

1½ pounds ricotta cheese
¼ pound toasted almonds, chopped
4 eggs
⅓ cup sugar
1 teaspoon vanilla extract
1 10-inch pie shell, strips of dough for lattice
    top
2 teaspoons confectioners' sugar

Rub the ricotta through a fine sieve and combine it with the almonds. Beat the eggs with the sugar until the mixture is foamy, and stir in the vanilla. Add the egg mixture to the cheese and beat until it is blended well. Turn the filling into the prepared pie shell and place the lattice strips over the top, pinching the edges together firmly. Bake the cheesecake in a moderate oven, 350° F., for 45 minutes, or until the filling is firm and the crust is done. At serving time, sprinkle with sugar. SERVES 10.

Fruitcake

PANFORTE DI SIENA

¼ pound almonds, coarsely chopped and
   lightly toasted
¼ pound hazelnuts, coarsely chopped and
   lightly toasted
⅓ cup unsweetened cocoa
4½ teaspoons cinnamon
¼ teaspoon allspice
½ cup flour
¾ cup candied orange peel, slivered
¾ cup candied citron, slivered
¾ cup candied lemon peel, slivered
¾ cup honey
¾ cup sugar
2 tablespoons confectioners' sugar

Combine the nuts, cocoa, 1½ teaspoons cinnamon, allspice, flour, and candied fruits. In a saucepan, combine the honey and sugar. Bring the mixture to a boil, and simmer until a little of the syrup dropped into cold water forms a soft ball. Add the fruit and nut mixture and mix well. Turn the mixture into a 9-inch spring-form pan lined with buttered paper, and bake in a slow oven, 300° F., for 30 minutes. Remove the bottom from the pan and cool the cake before removing the sides. Sprinkle with confectioners' sugar mixed with the remaining cinnamon. SERVES 10 TO 12.

Rum Icebox Cake

ZUPPA INGLESE

"Zuppa Inglese" means "English soup," a term that fails to describe this sweet favorite. It is similar to the English trifle, which perhaps eluded translation.

> 3 spongecake layers, 8 inches in diameter
> and ¾ inch high
> ⅔ cup dark rum
> 1 cup apricot or raspberry jam
> 4 cups Vanilla Cream (recipe below)
> 1½ cups cream, whipped
> Candied fruits

Place a spongecake layer on a platter, sprinkle it with ⅓ cup rum, and spread it with ½ cup jam and 2 cups

Vanilla Cream. Arrange the second layer on top, spread it with another ½ cup jam and 2 cups Vanilla Cream, and top with the remaining layer. Sprinkle on remaining rum and cover with whipped cream. Decorate the cake with candied fruits and chill it. SERVES 10 TO 12.

Vanilla Cream

CREMA ALLA VANIGLIA

6 eggs
¾ cup sugar
4 cups hot milk
¾ teaspoon vanilla

In the top of a double boiler, off the heat, beat the eggs, add sugar, and continue beating until the mixture is well blended. Gradually add hot milk, stirring with a whisk. Place the pan over simmering, but not boiling, water and cook for 6 to 7 minutes, stirring constantly with the whisk. When the custard thickens, remove from the heat, let it stand briefly in a pan of cold water, and stir in vanilla. Cool the custard before using in Zuppa Inglese.

Hot Wine Custard

ZABAGLIONE

Take great care, in cooking zabaglione, to beat constantly. And it is important not to let the ingredients get too hot. As in any other custard, the eggs may then separate. Do not try to make zabaglione without a double boiler; it is virtually impossible to get a smooth custard over direct heat.

8 egg yolks
2 egg whites
½ cup sugar
1 cup Marsala wine

In the top of a double boiler, off the heat, beat the egg yolks, egg whites, and sugar with a rotary or electric hand-beater until the mixture is very thick and creamy. Add the wine; place the pan over simmering (not boiling) water and heat the mixture, beating constantly, until it is hot and thick. Serve it in stemmed glasses. If desired, serve a few berries in the bottom of each glass. Serve with spongecake or ladyfingers. SERVES 4.

Anise Cookies with Pine Nuts

BISCOTTI ALL'ANICE

2 whole eggs
4 egg yolks
1 cup sugar
2½ cups sifted cake flour
2 teaspoons anise extract
Pine nuts

Beat the whole eggs, egg yolks, and sugar until the mixture is light and foamy. Blend in the cake flour and anise extract. Drop by the teaspoonful on buttered cooky sheets, leaving about an inch between cookies. Decorate the cookies with pine nuts. Bake in a moderately hot oven, 375° F., for 12 minutes, or until the cookies are light brown. MAKES ABOUT 3 DOZEN COOKIES.

Macaroons

AMARETTI

⅔ cup blanched almonds
2 egg whites
½ cup fine granulated sugar
½ teaspoon almond extract

Put the almonds twice through the finest blade of the food chopper. Beat the egg whites until stiff and add the sugar gradually, beating constantly. Add the almonds and the almond extract and drop by teaspoonfuls on a buttered baking sheet 1½ inches apart. Bake in a moderately slow oven, 300° F., for 12 to 15 minutes, or until the cookies are brown. MAKES ABOUT 2 DOZEN COOKIES.

Meringues

MERINGHE

4 egg whites
Pinch of salt
¼ teaspoon almond extract
¼ teaspoon cream of tartar
1 cup fine sugar

Beat egg whites with a pinch of salt and the almond extract until the egg whites are stiff but not dry. Beat in the cream of tartar and the sugar a tablespoon at a time. Put the meringue in a pastry bag and force it through to a buttered baking sheet, making shells about the size of a large egg. Bake for 30 minutes in a very slow oven, 250° F. The meringues should be stiff but should not turn color. If desired, serve the meringues with ice cream. MAKES ABOUT 8 MERINGUES.

Sweet Knots

The Sweet Knots make their appearance in Tuscany for the Shrove Tuesday celebration.

    3 eggs
    2 tablespoons sugar
        Pinch of salt
    1 tablespoon brandy
    2 cups sifted flour
 1½ teaspoons baking powder
    2 tablespoons butter, softened
        Deep hot fat
        Confectioners' sugar

Beat the eggs with the sugar, salt, and brandy until the mixture is frothy. Sift the flour with the baking powder and then gradually add it to the eggs. Work the butter into the mixture. The dough should be soft, but add a little flour if necessary to make it stiff enough to knead. Knead the dough on a lightly floured board until it is smooth; cover it and let the dough rest for 1 hour. Divide the dough in half and roll out each half into a thin rectangle. Cut the dough into strips about 1 inch wide and 5 inches long; knot the strips and set them aside for 10 minutes. Fry the knots, a few at a time, in deep hot fat, 370° F., until they are light golden. Sprinkle with confectioners' sugar. If desired, serve the Cenci with whipped cream. SERVES 8.

INDEX

Index